Dedicated to Savy and Peanut, who make every day an adventure. Thank you for traveling the world with us.

BRAZIL

Educational Resources, Crafts & Activities for Kids

Sarah M. Prowant, MSN-Ed, RN

Savy Activities
Colorado, USA

Savy Activities© All Rights Reserved

TERMS & CONDITIONS

This product is licensed for single use only (single home or classroom). Redistributing, selling, editing or sharing any part of this product in any part thereof is strictly forbidden without the written permission of Savy Activities. You may make copies for your personal use but will need to purchase separate licenses for use in additional classrooms and/or schools. Failure to comply is a legal copyright infringement and will be prosecuted to the full extent of the law.

When posting photos of any part of this product on social media, please give credit to "Savy Activities" by hyperlinking to our website and tagging us as @SavyActivities on social media.

We reserve the right to change this policy at any time. If you have any questions regarding this or other of our materials, please contact us directly.

FOR BEST RESULTS:

 When assembling a 3D model, glue a second piece of thick paper with a craft glue stick to back of each sheet of model pieces (prior to cutting pieces) to provide additional stability when assembled.

 Laminate all cards & posters with at least 3 ml lamination for additional protection.

 If printing from an ebook, cardstock paper (>60 lbs) provides best results for cards, models and manipulative activities, while standard printer paper is adequate for recipes, lessons, etc. Please set printer to "FIT TO PAGE" when printing for best results.

FOLLOW US ON SOCIAL MEDIA!

 @savyactivities

 /SavyActivities

www.SavyActivities.com

WHATS INCLUDED:

- Educational Brazil Poster & Flag
- Brazil Landmark Three-Part Cards
- Brazil Cities & Landmarks Map Pinning
- Brazil Federative States & Colonization History
- South America Continent Brazil Flag Pinning & Outline
- Brazil Fun Facts
- Brazil History Timeline Poster
- Brazil Coat of Arms & National Anthem
- Christ the Redeemer Model
- Brazilian Traditional Dress Dolls
- Brazil Fauna Three-Part Cards
- Saci-Pererê Minibook
- Football Pitch Poster & Activity
- Bumba Meu Boi Play
- Carnival Headdress Craft
- Toilet Roll Ganzá
- Portuguese Language Cards
- Brigadeiros Recipe
- Life Cycle, Tracing, Parts of Coffee
- Amazon River Habitat Matching & Tributaries Tracing
- Parts of River Matching & Feature Cards
- Meeting of the Waters & River Erosion Experiments
- Macaw Handprint Craft
- Anaconda Craft
- Snakes of the Amazon Cards
- Clothespin Piranhas Craft
- Counting Clip Cards
- Brazil Currency Real R$
- Indigenous Tribes of the Amazon Info Cards
- Rede Hammock Craft
- Kayapo Design Tracing
- Asháninka Palm Crown Craft

Brazil

National Flora: Ipê-amarelo
National Fauna: Jaguar
Capital City: Brasilia
Currency: Brazilian Real R$
Language: Portuguese
National Holiday(s): September 7

Famous Landmarks:

Christ The Redeemer
Sugarloaf Mountain
Museum of Art of São Paulo
Cathedral of Brasília
Museu do Amanhã
Iguazu Falls
Niterói Art Museum
Amazon River

Brazil

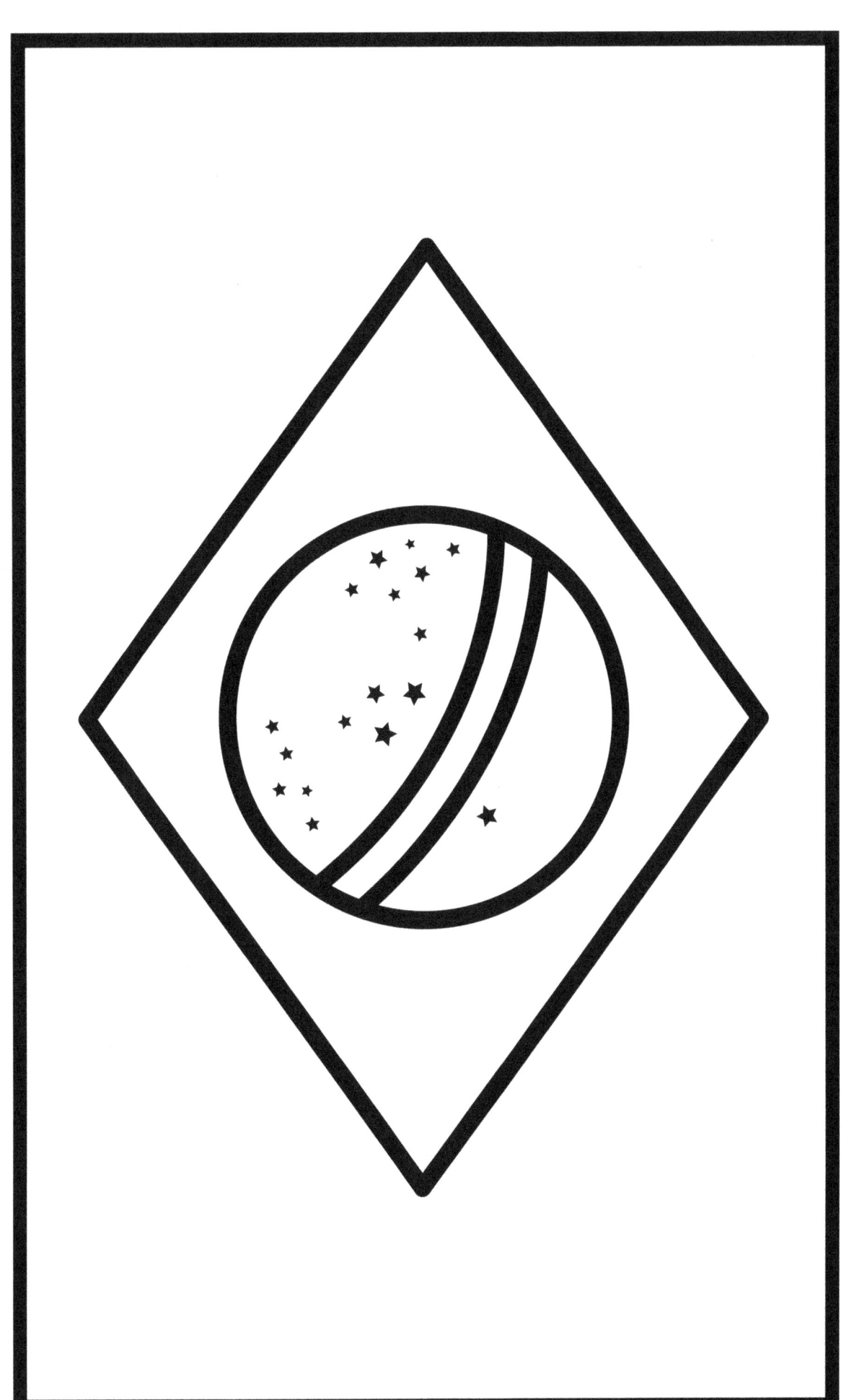

Brazil Flag Coloring Page

Brazil Landmarks (3-Part Cards)

Christ The Redeemer

Sugarloaf Mountain

Museum of Art of São Paulo

Cathedral of Brasília

Brazil Landmarks (3-Part Cards)

Christ The Redeemer

Sugarloaf Mountain

Museum of Art of São Paulo

Cathedral of Brasília

Brazil Landmarks (3-Part Cards)

Museu do Amanhã

Iguazu Falls

Niterói Contemporary Art Museum

Amazon River

Brazil Landmarks (3-Part Cards)

Museu do Amanhã

Iguazu Falls

Niterói Contemporary Art Museum

Amazon River

Brazil Landmarks

Cut out circles using a 1" circle punch or scissors. Place circles on map where the landmarks are located. Refer to the control version for help if needed.

Brazil Cities

Cut out the labels and attach them to the diagram

Rio de Janeiro	São Paulo	Manaus	Belo Horizonte
Curitiba	Porto Alegre	Salvador	Brasilia
Recife			
Fortaleza			
Goiânia			
São Luís			

Instructions

Paste included map illustration onto foamboard, cardboard or corkboard. Glue straight or T-pin to back of labels or photo circles and pin into map at appropriate location of landmark or city.

Brazil

Brazil
Federative States

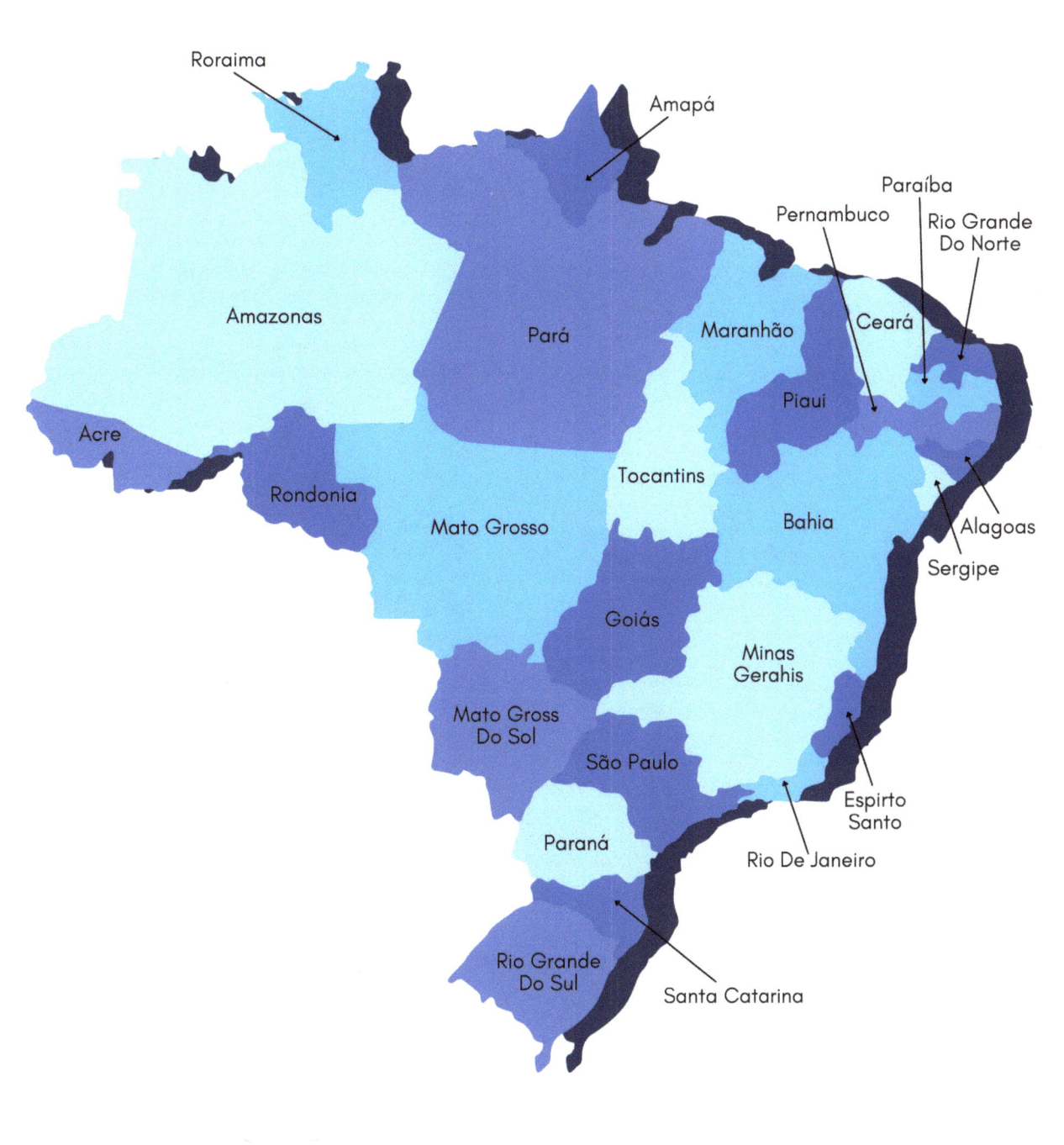

Colonization of Brazil

In 1498, Vasco da Gama successfully sailed from Portugal to India, around southern Africa, establishing an overseas route between Europe and Asia, a feat Columbus had failed to accomplish a few years previous. In 1500, Pedro Alvares Cabral attempted the same voyage, but veered west and landed on the shores of Brazil. This discovery lead to the establishment of fifteen colonies in 1534, and Portuguese colonization began to over overtake native lands. Resources such as brazilwood, sugar and gold were exploited and slave trade established. During the following centuries, indigenous people were gradually dispossessed of their land as colonization continued to spread across the continent.

Cut out the included maps. Color the political borders if desired. Layer the pages so the smallest page is on the top and the largest page is on the bottom, making sure each date or date range is visible on each tab. Staple all the sheets together to form a small flip book. Compare and contrast geographical regions at different years; what changes occurred at these times?

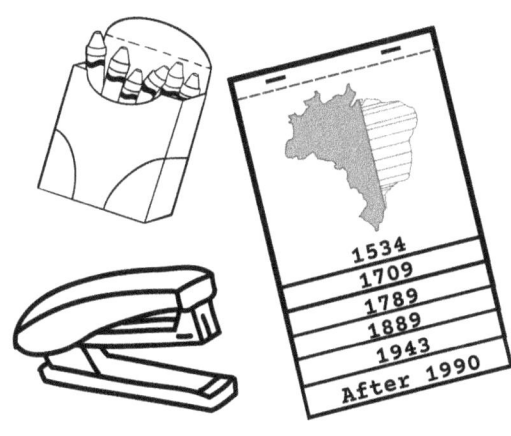

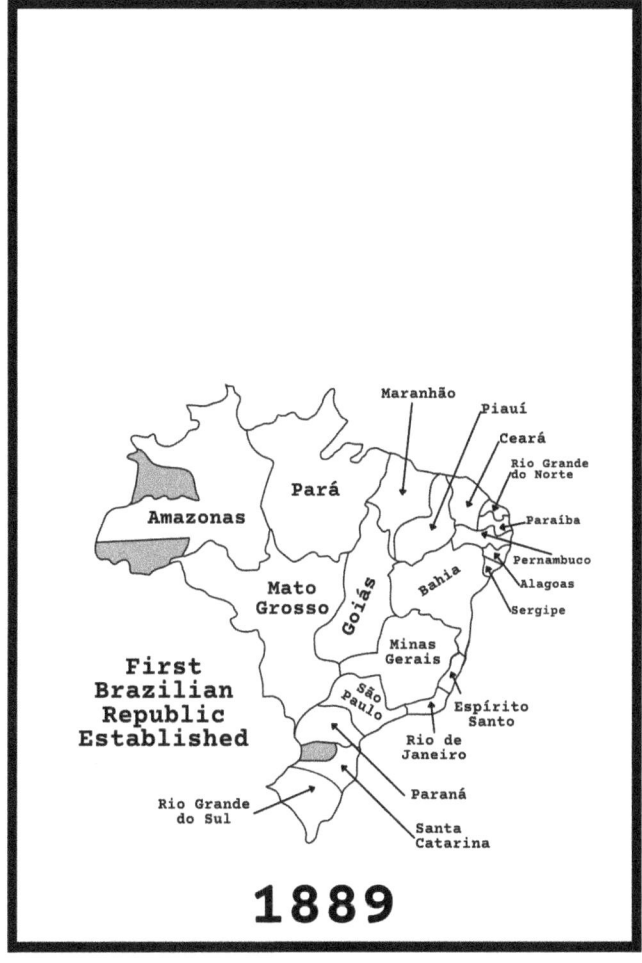

1889

1789

1534

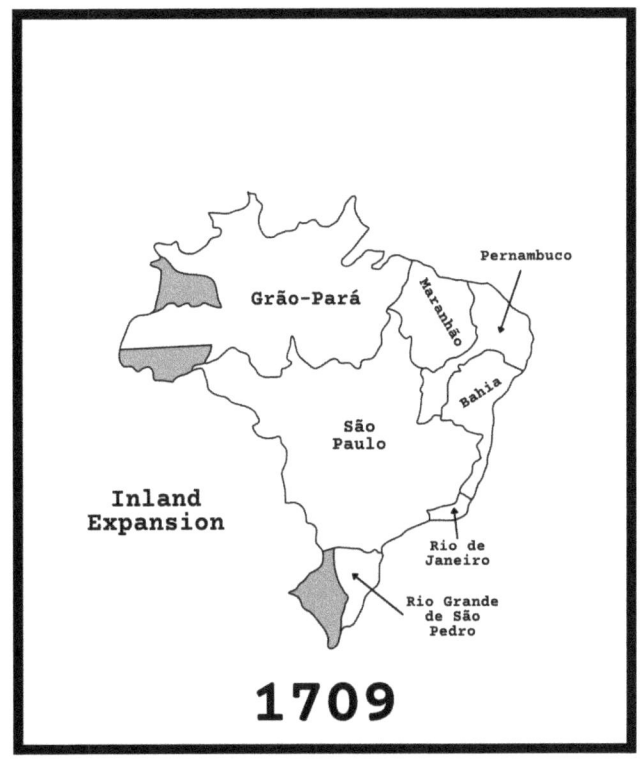

1709

After 1990

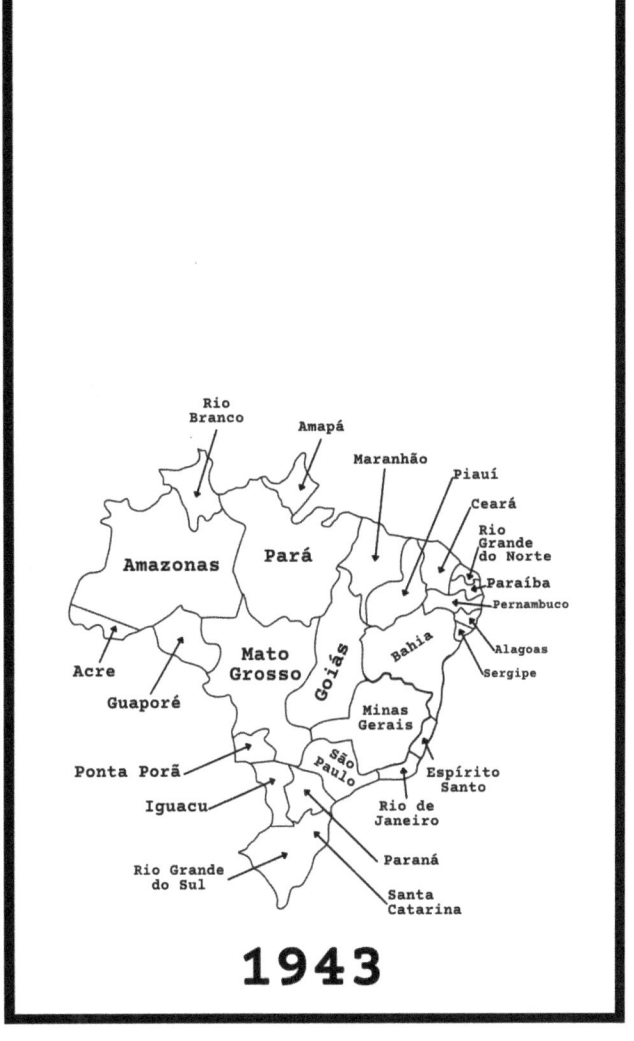

1943

South America Continent: Brazil

Cut out South America continent. Glue over corkboard or cardboard. Cut out flag and glue onto toothpick or straight pin. Mark country with flag.

Brazil Fun Facts

José Braz Araripe of Brazil developed the automatic transmission in cars In 1932.

The Brazilian football (soccer) team have won the world cup a record 15 times

Rio de Janeiro was once the capital of Portugal, making it the only European capital to be located outside Europe.

Queimada Grande Island has about 45 venomous snakes per 328 feet, and is known as snake island.

Along the Amazon are over 100 tribes that have never had contact with outside civilization.

The starry night on the flag is based on the night of November 15, 1889, as seen from Rio de Janeiro.

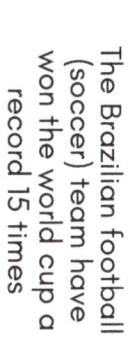

Rio de Janeiro hosts the world's largest carnival (over 6 million people), celebrated in March.

Brazil has more animal and plant species than any other country in the world.

Brazil Fun Facts

The Amazon is the world's largest tropical rainforest, covering about 8 million square km's of Brazil.

Voting is mandatory in Brazil, requiring all citizens between 18 and 70 to participate in elections.

Cashew of Pirangi is the biggest cashew tree in the world, covering over 73,000 square meters.

Brazil is home to *Neonothopanus gardneri*, locally known as *flor de coco*, a glow in the dark fungus.

Brazil is the only country in South America that speaks Portuguese.

Brazil is the largest country in South America.

Brazil has been the largest producer of coffee for the last 150 years.

The name Brazil comes from a tree named brazilwood.

Brazil Coat of Arms

Brazil National Anthem

The placid banks of the Ipiranga
Heard the resounding cry of a heroic people,
And brilliant beams from the sun of liberty
Shone in our homeland's skies at that very moment.
If with strong arms we have succeeded
In winning the pledge of equality,
In thy bosom, O freedom,
Our brave breast shall defy death itself!

O beloved,
Idolized homeland,
Hail, hail!

Brazil, an intense dream, a vivid ray
Of love and hope descends to earth,
If in thy lovely, smiling and clear skies
The image of the Southern Cross shines resplendently.
A giant by thine own nature,
Thou art a beautiful, strong and fearless colossus,
And thy future mirrors thy greatness.

Beloved Land,
Amongst a thousand others
Art thou, Brazil,
O beloved homeland!
To the sons of this land
Thou art a gentle mother,
Beloved homeland,
Brazil!

Laid out eternally in a splendid cradle,
By the sound of the sea and the light of the deep sky,
Thou shinest, O Brazil, the finial of America,
Illuminated by the sun of the New World!
Thy smiling, lovely fields have more flowers
Than the most elegant land abroad,
Our woods have more life,
Our life in thy bosom more love.

O beloved,
Idolized homeland,
Hail, hail!

Brazil, let the star-spangled banner thou showest forth
Be the symbol of eternal love,
And let the green-gold of thy pennant proclaim:
– Peace in the future and glory in the past.
But if thou raisest the strong mace of justice,
Thou wilt see that a son of thine flees not from battle,
Nor does he who loves thee fear death itself.

Beloved Land,
Amongst a thousand others
Art thou, Brazil,
O beloved homeland!
To the sons of this land
Thou art a gentle mother,
Beloved homeland,
Brazil!

CHRIST THE REDEEMER MODEL

Instructions

Christ the Redeemer is the iconic statute of Rio de Janeiro, Brazil, and overlooks the Tijuca Forest National Park. The statue is 30 meters (98 feet) high, and the arms stretch 28 meters (92 feet) wide. It was built in the early 1900's and has become a cultural icon of both Rio de Janeiro and Brazil.

Materials
- Christ the Redeemer Template
- Scissors
- Glue or Tape
- Clothespins (Optional)

Cut out the included illustrations. Glue the front and the back of the statue by applying glue on the head and arms. Keep in place by using clothespins. Allow to dry thoroughly. Assemble base by folding on indicated lines and gluing tabs inside. Tape can also be used or hot glue if desired for quicker assembly. To complete statute, fold the base of the statue with included tabs to form a circular base. Glue (or tape) into place. Trim bottom of statute if needed. Secure to base and allow to dry completely.

Discuss: What views would be visible from different parts of Rio de Janeiro?

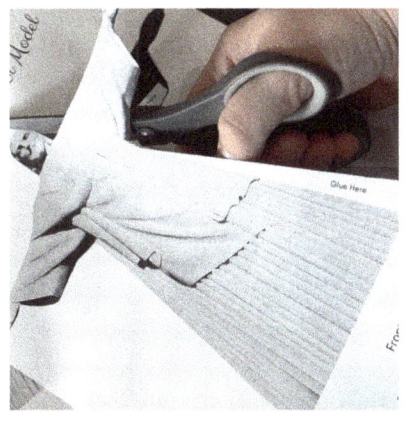  
 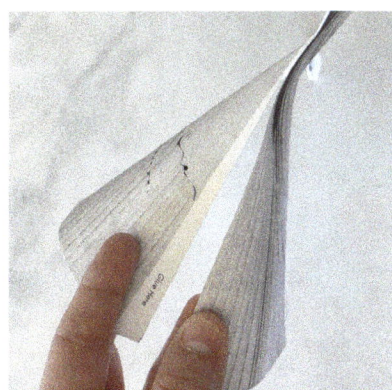 

Christ the Redeemer Model

Front
Glue Here

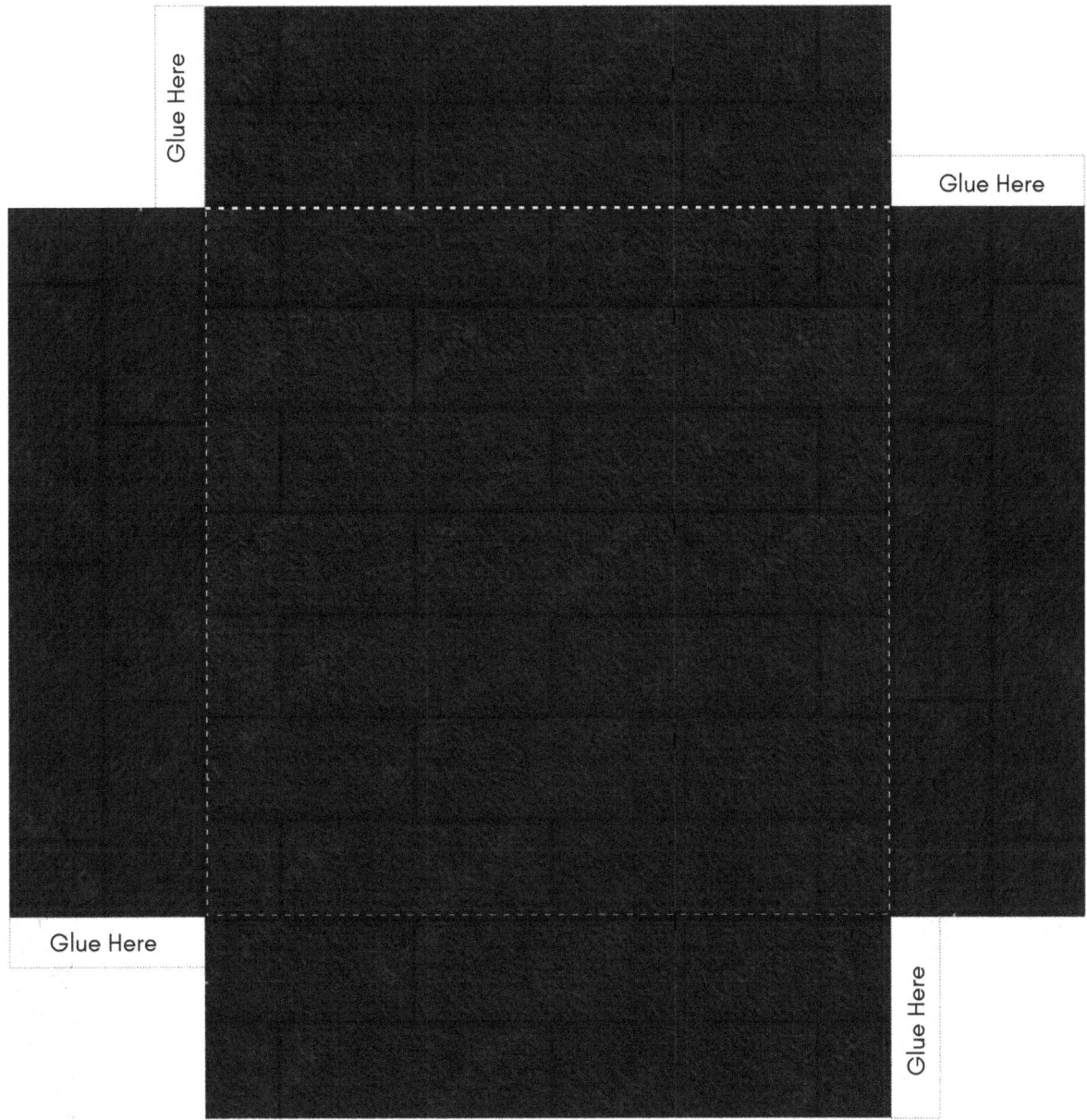

Base

Brazilian Traditional Dress

Brazil Fauna (3-Part Cards)

Macaw **Tapir**

Pink River Dolphin **Sloth**

Brazil Fauna (3-Part Cards)

Macaw **Tapir**

Pink River Dolphin **Sloth**

Brazil Fauna (3-Part Cards)

Bearded Tamarin

Jaguar

Giant Anteater

Piranha

Brazil Fauna (3-Part Cards)

Bearded Tamarin

Jaguar

Giant Anteater

Piranha

SACI-PERERÊ

Saci's job is to protect the forest, but he is also known for being a prankster. His hat gives him the power to disappear.

Saci is so popular in Brazil that he is celebrated on Saci Day, which is in October each year.

Deep in the forests of Brazil, lives a little boy named Saci-Pererê. He has only one leg and wears a red cap.

1

So, if you ever visit Brazil and have funny things happen, you can be sure they are probably the work of a little boy named Saci-Pererê.

THE END.

10

Saci enjoys pranking people, but most of his pranks are harmless. Whenever accidents happen, Saci-Pererê is usually to blame.

3

Saci loves to juggle and spends many afternoons juggling different things he's collected.

8

Sometimes people try to steal Saci's hat. This causes him to loose his powers, and makes him very sad. He often will grant wishes in exchange for the return of his hat.

7

Having only one leg doesn't prevent Saci from moving around; he can be seen whirling by in a mini tornado!

4

Assembly Instructions

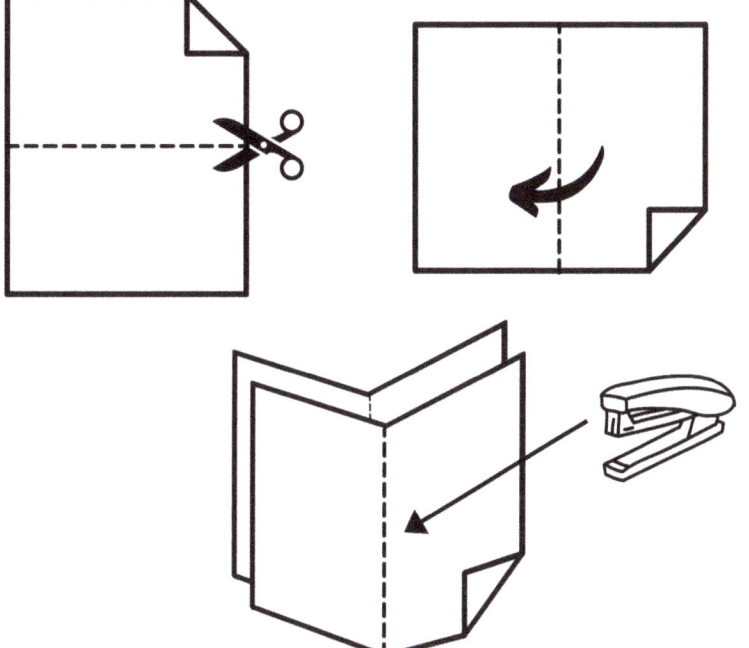

Cut paper in half on lines. Fold each page of book as indicated. Collate together so pages match up appropriately. Staple spine to hold together.

Sometimes people come into the forest to cut down trees. Saci doesn't like to see his forest destroyed.

Saci doesn't hurt the people, but he plays such annoying tricks on them, that most of them don't come back.

Football Pitch
(Soccer Field)

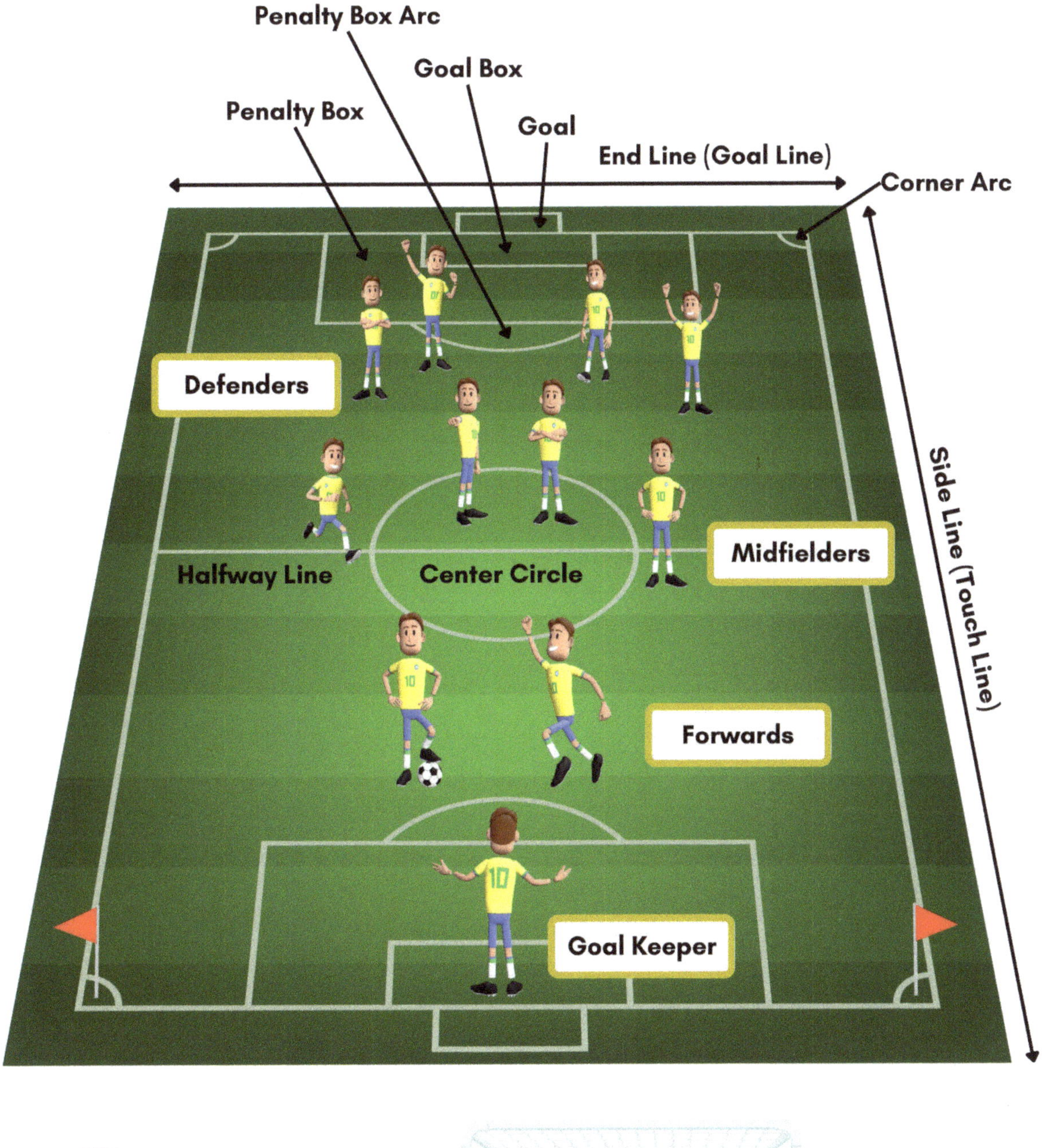

- Penalty Box Arc
- Goal Box
- Penalty Box
- Goal
- End Line (Goal Line)
- Corner Arc
- Defenders
- Halfway Line
- Center Circle
- Midfielders
- Side Line (Touch Line)
- Forwards
- Goal Keeper

Ball
68–70 cm (27–28 in)
410–450 g (14–16 oz)

Net
7.32 m Wide (24 ft)
2.44 m High (8 ft)
1.5 m Deep (5 ft)

FOOTBALL (SOCCER)

Instructions

Football (known as Soccer in the United States), is a very important sport to the Brazilian culture. It is known around the world as *Seleção Brasileira de Futebol*, though sometimes they are just referred to as *Seleção*. Historically, this team is the best, winning the FIFA World Cup five times, and the best overall performance in the World Cup competitions.

Materials
- Soccer Ball
- Flat Outdoor Surface
- Goals

Football is a team sport, played with a spherical ball between two teams of 11 players. The two teams compete to get the ball into the other team's goal (between the posts and under the bar), thereby scoring a goal. Players are not allowed to touch the ball with hands or arms while it is in play, except for the goalkeepers within the penalty area. Players may use any other part of their body to strike or pass the ball, and mainly use their feet. The team that scores more goals at the end of the game is the winner.

BUMBA MEU BOI

Instructions

Bumba Meu Boi is an interactive play celebrated in Brazil. Originating in the 18th century, this play is a form of social criticism. Lower class Brazilians mock and criticize those of higher social status through a comedic folklore story told in song and dance. There are many variations of the play with alternative story lines, but the principle themes remain the same.

Materials
- Theater & Puppet Pieces
- Scissors
- Glue (or Tape)
- Clothespins (optional)
- Story Screenplay

Cut out included theater and puppet templates. Carefully cut out the inside of the theater front - an adult may need to assist with this step. Fold each piece along dashed lines, as indicated. Secure background scene to side pieces with tabs on outside. Repeat with front of theater so a rectangle structure is formed. Clothespins may be helpful to hold pieces in place while drying if glue is used. Secure the marquee to the front of the theater. Next, adjust (and trim if needed) the finger puppets to fit the child's finger-size. Place theater on the edge of a surface so the child's hand can fit inside from bottom. Secure to surface with tabs on side. Perform the show!

 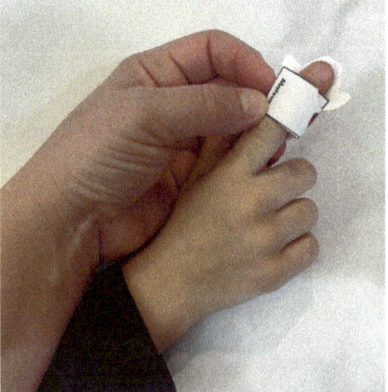 

BUMBA MEU BOI
Screenplay

Narrator: Once upon a time, a couple named Catirina and Mateus were pregnant with their first child. Mateus worked hard on a nearby farm, owned by Cavalo Marinho.
Cavalo Marinho: What a wonderful farm I have!
Sebastião & Mateus: *together* That's because we do all the work around here!
Narrator: One day, Catirina started craving something weird - the tongue of an ox!
Catirina: Mateus, I need to find an ox tongue to eat; I really believe if I don't get an ox tongue, my baby will be harmed!
Mateus: I will see if I can find one for you.
Narrator: Mateus didn't know where to find his wife an ox tongue. Finally he decided to kill an ox at the farm he worked at, and take the tongue to his wife.
Mateus: *Hits ox*
Ox: Moooooooo!!
Narrator: What Mateus didn't know was the ox he killed was Cavalo Marinho's favorite.
Cavalo Marinho: *sees dead ox* Who killed my favorite ox? I am going to throw whoever did this in jail!
Sebastião: It wasn't me!
Mateus: I'm sorry, I killed the ox - I was trying to get an ox tongue for my pregnant wife Catirina, it's all she wants!
Cavalo Marinho: I don't care what your reason was, you killed MY ox! You will pay!
Mateus: Wait! Let's have a Pajé see if he can bring the ox back to life.
Cavalo Marinho: That's ridiculous, there is nobody that can fix the damage you have done!
Catirina: Please let the Pajé try, I can't raise this baby alone!
Pajé: *mumbles, waving hands*
Ox: Moooo!
Cavalo Marinho: It's a miracle! My ox is alive, so I will forgive you for what you did.
Catirina & Mateus: Thank you!
Narrator: And Catirina and Mateus lived happily ever after.

CARNIVAL HEADDRESS

Instructions

Carnival of Brazil is an annual Brazilian festival held the Friday before Ash Wednesday, which marks the beginning of Lent, the forty-day period before Easter. Headdresses are frequently worn by Carnival dancers, and include a solid headband decorated with feathers and embellishments.

Materials
- Headdress Template
- Scissors
- Markers or Crayons
- Glue or Tape
- Craft Feathers (Optional)

Decorate the included template by coloring with crayons or markers on both the headband and the feathers. Cut out the pieces and glue to inside of peaked band. Allow to dry thoroughly. For added realism, use craft feathers instead of included paper feathers. After completely dry, use the second part of band and glue to form banded circle. Adjust to child's head size. Add additional embellishments if desired.

Discuss: What are some other holidays and celebrations that traditionally wear head decorations? What countries are they celebrated in?

TOILET ROLL GANZÁ

Instructions

The ganzá is a Brazilian rattle used as a percussion instrument, especially in Samba music. The ganzá is cylindrically shaped, and can be either a hand-woven basket or a metal canister which is filled with beads, metal balls, pebbles, or other similar items. Those made from metal produce a particularly loud sound. They are usually used to play a rhythm underneath the rest of the band.

Cut out included ganzá templates. Glue one end over end of a toilet roll, securing the tabs to the roll with glue or tape. Allow to dry completely. Fill tube with dry beans or corn. Glue opposite end onto roll and allow to dry completely. Wrap center piece around tube securing it with tab in middle and encircling the tube completely. Secure with tape or glue and trim to fit.

Suggestion: Listen to samba music and shake the ganzá along to the beat.

Materials

- Ganzá Templates
- Toilet Roll
- Scissors
- Tape (or Glue)
- Dry Beans or Corn

Toilet Roll Ganzá

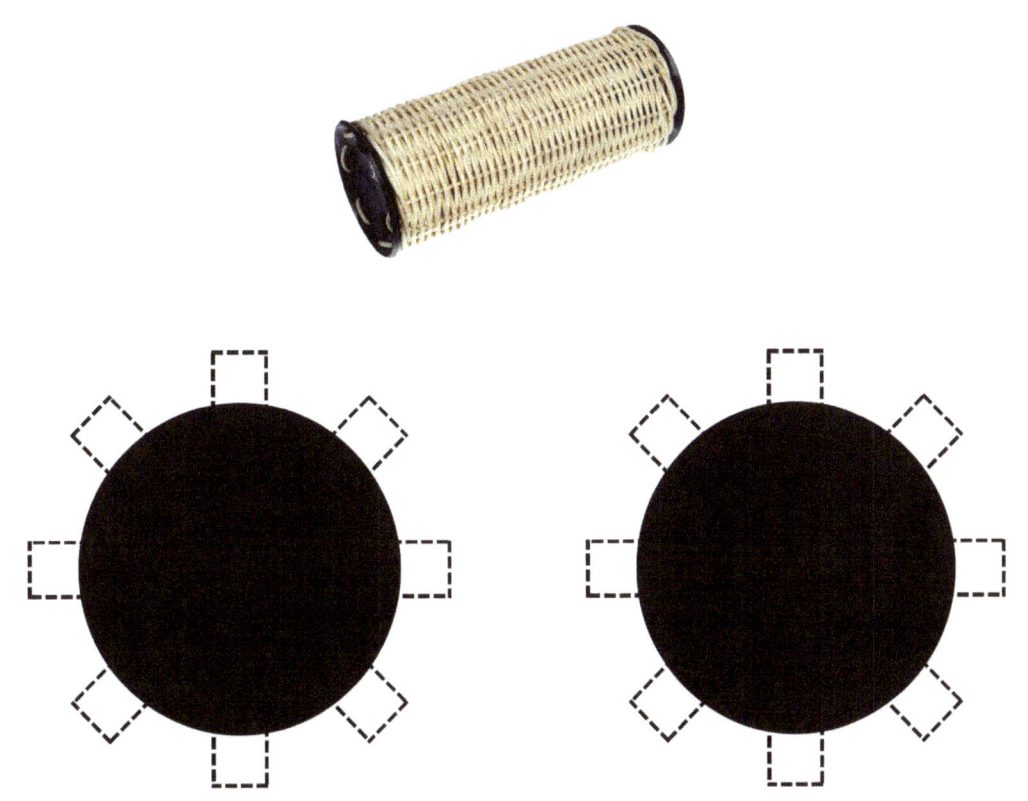

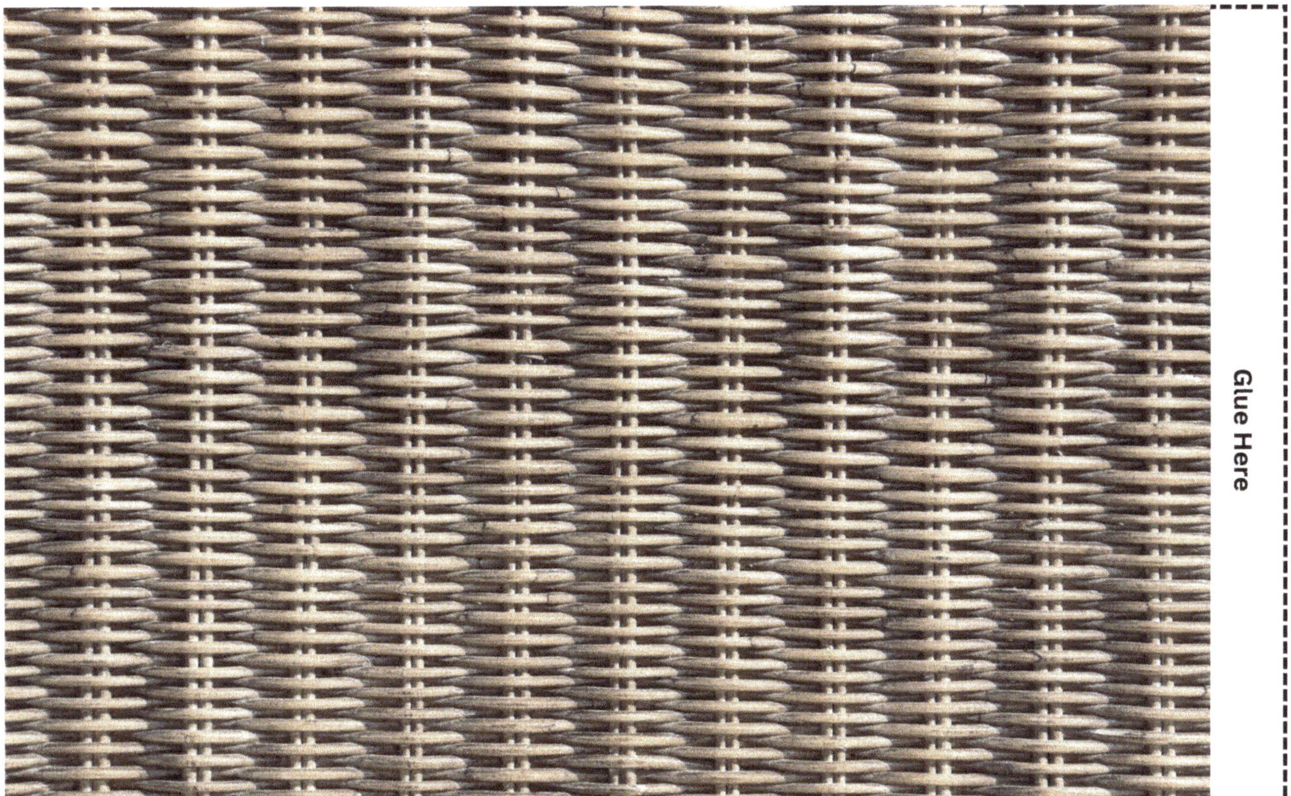

Portuguese Language Cards

Hello

Goodbye

See you later!

My name is _____

Portuguese Language Cards

Como vai você?
How are you?

E ai?
What's up?

Desculpe

I'm Sorry

Fica à vonta de
Make yourself feel at home

BRIGADEIROS

ingredients

- 1 Tablespoon Butter
- 14 Ounces Sweetened Condensed Milk
- ¼ Cup Cocoa Powder
- 1 Cup Chocolate Sprinkles

directions

- In a medium pot over low heat, melt together butter, condensed milk, and cocoa powder, stirring continuously until mixture becomes moderately thickened.
- Pour into a greased casserole dish, and chill for 1 hour in refrigerator.
- Shape and roll the chilled mixture into balls.
- Roll the balls in chocolate sprinkles.

Brigadeiros

INGREDIENTS

BUTTER

CONDENSED MILK, SWEETENED

COCOA POWDER

CHOCOLATE SPRINKLES

Life Cycle Spinner

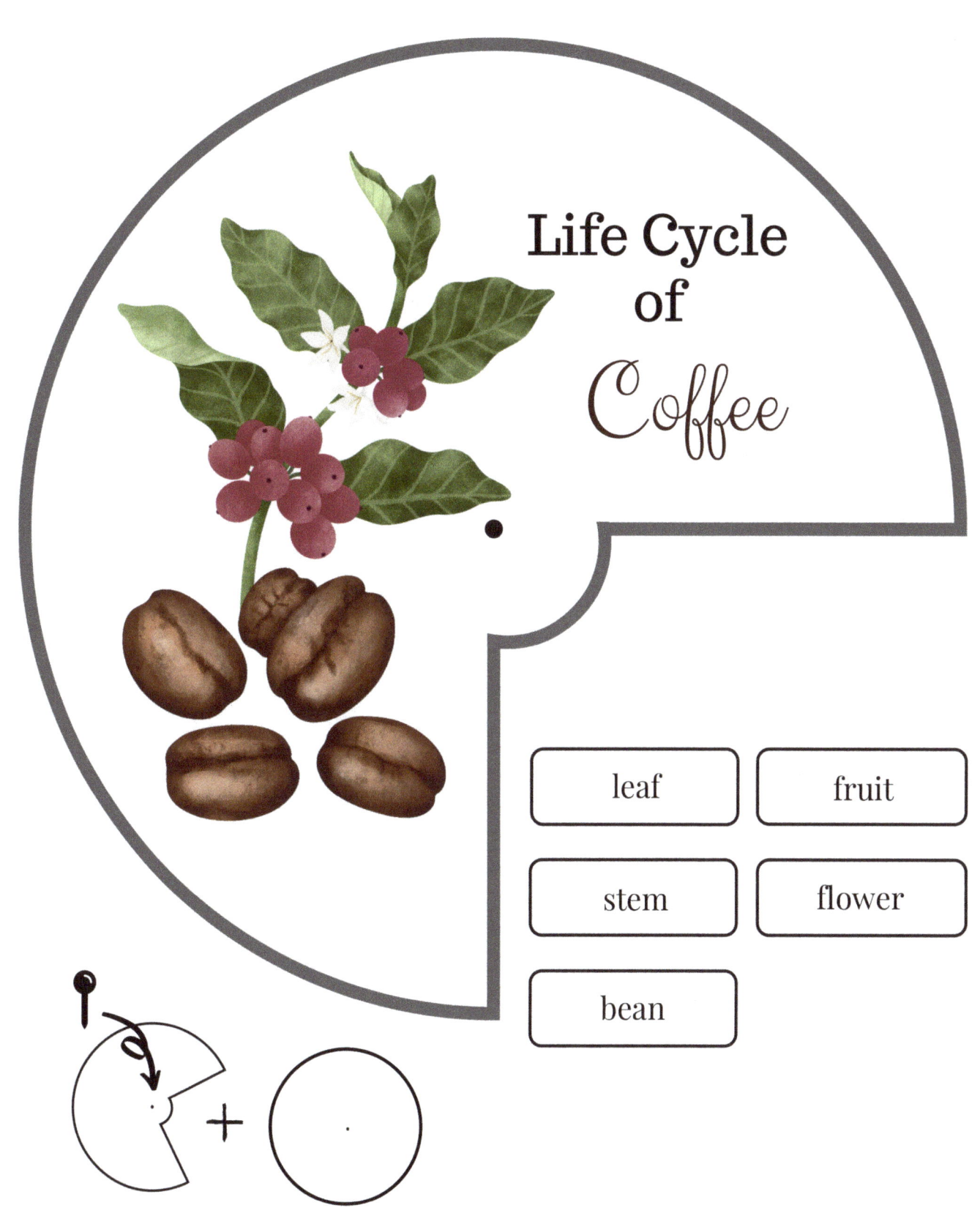

Life Cycle of Coffee

leaf | fruit
stem | flower
bean

Life Cycle Spinner

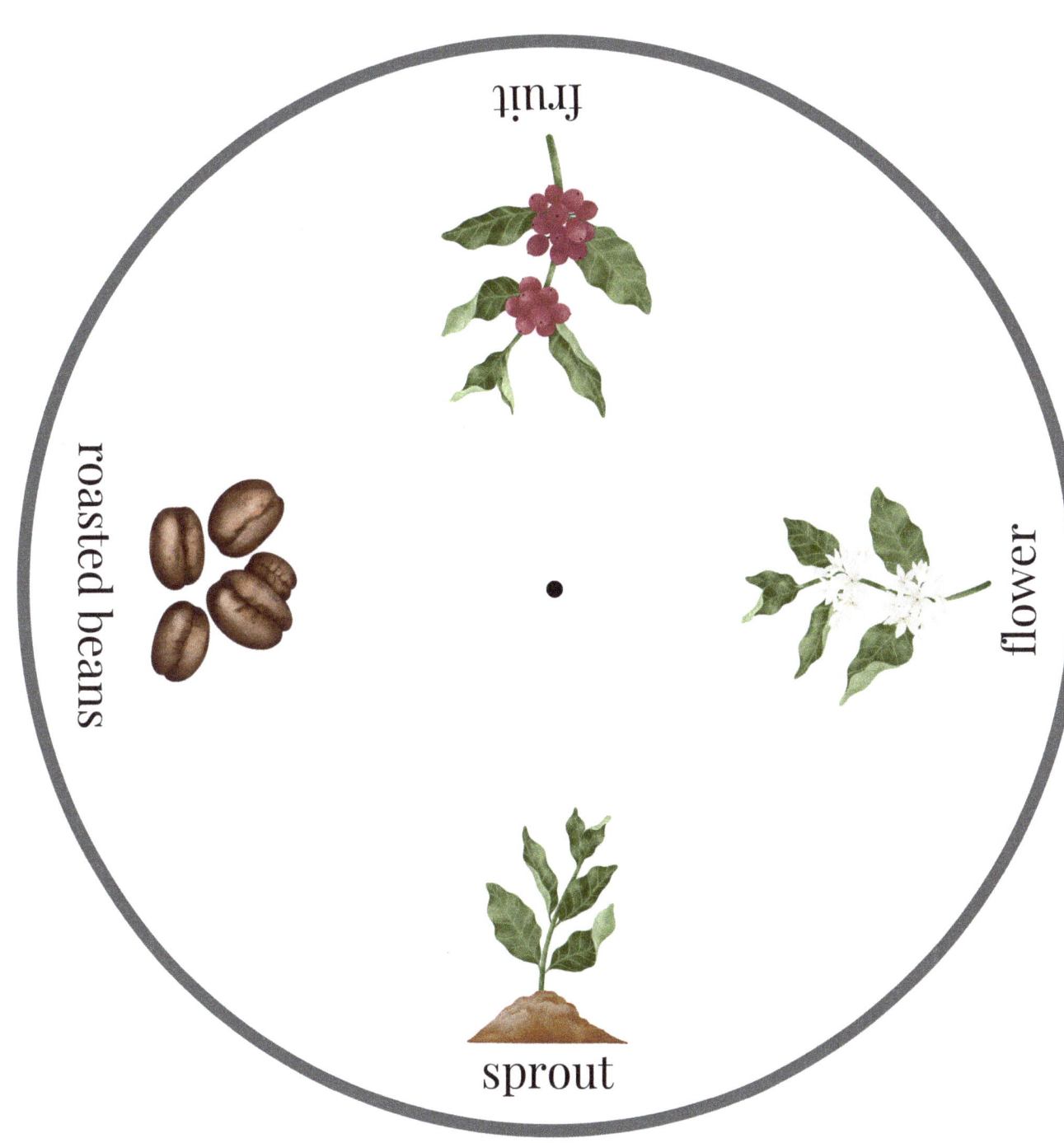

Parts of the Coffee Plant

Learning to Write

River Habitat Matching

Cut out circles of animals and match into appropriate habitat.

Amazon River Habitat

Climate

The climate of Amazonia is warm, rainy, and humid, with heavy rain alternating with clear, sunny days. In the lower reaches of the river basin, cooling winds blow most of the year.

Flora

The Amazon River is home to the giant water lilies, which can grow up to 10 feet (or 3 meters) in diameter and can hold up to 60 pounds of weight. Much of the plant life of the Amazon has adapted to thriving underwater during the rainy seasons.

Fauna

The Amazon River is home to a plethora of mammals, reptiles and amphibians. Some of the most notable are the pink river dolphin, giant river otter, carnivorous fish, and green anaconda.

Water

The Amazon is responsible for about 20% of the Earth's fresh water entering the ocean. The water is discolored by sediment and decayed leaf and plant matter. There is a noticeable difference when the different compositions "mix".

Parts of a River

1.
2.
3.
4.
5.
6.
7.
8.
9.
10.
11.
12.
13.
14.
15.

Parts of a River

Source	Stream
Glacier	Lake
Tributary	Waterfall
Confluence	Meander
Levee	Marsh
Floodplain	Delta
Distributary	Mouth
	Ocean

Amazon River Tributaries Tracing

Amazon River Features Cards

Amazon River Features Cards

MEETING OF THE WATERS EXPERIMENT

Materials
- Large Casserole Dish
- Dark Cooking Oil
- Water
- Cocoa Powder
- Flour

Instructions

The *Meeting of Waters* is the confluence between the dark *Rio Negro* and the upper portion of the pale sandy-colored *Amazon River* (*Solimões River*). For over 6 km (3.7 miles) the two rivers flow side by side without mixing. It is one of the main tourist attractions of Manaus, Brazil.

Mix 2 cups water with 1 teaspoon of cocoa powder and 1/2 teaspoon of flour to create muddy looking water. Measure 2 cups of a dark cooking oil (sesame or grape seed oil works well) in a separate container. Pour both oil and cocoa-water into a large casserole dish simultaneously and observe how they interact with one another. Attempt to mix the two mixtures together and observe the outcome.

Discuss: What happens when the oil and cocoa-water are mixed? What does the mixture look like in 5 minutes? 10 minutes? The *Meeting of the Waters* phenomenon is due to the differences in temperature, speed, and amount of dissolved sediments in the waters of the two rivers. Although this experiment mimics the interaction of this confluence, it is due to different variables - can you describe why these two solutions do not mix?

RIVER EROSION EXPERIMENT

Instructions

A river forms from water moving from a higher elevation to a lower elevation, all due to gravity. When rain falls on the land, it either seeps into the ground or becomes runoff, which flows downhill into rivers and lakes, on its journey towards the sea. This science experiment demonstrates how rivers flow through the path of least resistance until it reaches the bottom.

Materials
- Soil
- Rocks
- Water
- Two Casserole Dishes

Fill a casserole dish with dirt. Include a few stones in to see how the river affects them. Make sure the dirt is moist and packed into dish. Angle the casserole dish into a second dish (gravity). Lightly pour water onto a spot at the top and observe the water erode the dirt creating a riverbed. Be careful to not pour the water too fast, as this will erode too much.

Discuss: How do obstacles such as stones affect the river path? Is the river straight or does it have bends?

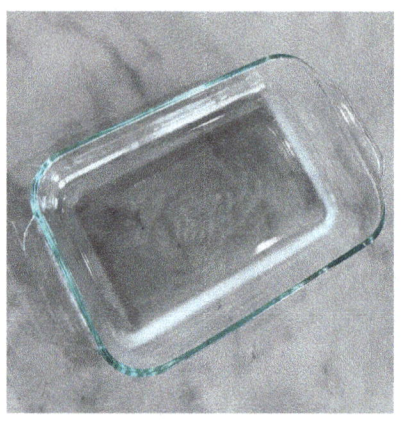  

MACAW HANDPRINT CRAFT

Instructions

The macaw is a colorful bird known for their long tails and vibrant feathers. They are native to Southern North America and South American, specifically tropical rainforests and similar habitats. Brazil has several species of macaws that are native and endemic to the country. Unfortunately, many are facing extinction due to deforestation and poaching.

Materials
- Macaw Pattern
- Colored Construction Paper
- Scissors
- Glue Stick
- Googly Eye

Cut out included macaw pattern. Use pattern to trace onto stiff colored paper. Choose one color for main body and contrasting colors for eyepatch, beak and feet. Trace child's hand on 3-5 sheets of construction paper. Using glue stick, adhere the eye patch, beak and feet to the macaw body. Layer the handprints to form feathers. Add a googly eye to complete the craft.

Discuss: What colors of feathers do macaw have? How do the colors vary between species?

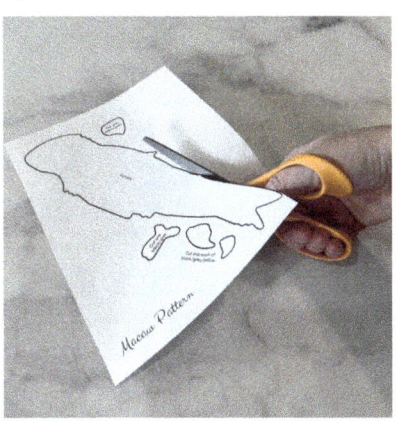

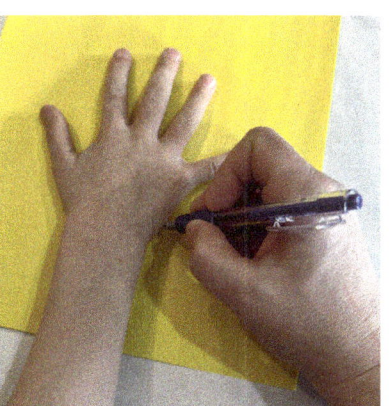

ANACONDA CRAFT

Instructions

Anacondas are one of the world's heaviest and longest snakes, often reaching 150 lbs in adult males and measuring up to 20 feet long. Although they are nonvenomous and primarily aquatic, they eat a wide variety of prey, almost anything they can manage to overpower, crush and swallow.

Cut out the included anaconda illustration. Cut snake around circular lines. Cut out included tongue and glue or tape onto underside of snake. Using a hole punch, cut a hole on the "tail" portion of the snake, as illustrated. Thread a small length of string or yarn through the hole and tie securely. Hang snake from doorway or ceiling with optional thumbtack.

Discuss: Measure the length of the paper snake in it's coiled position, how long do you think it is? How long is it? How does that compare to a larger snake in the wild?

Materials
- Anaconda Illustration
- Scissors
- Tape (or Glue)
- Hole Punch
- String or Yarn
- Thumbtack (optional)

Anaconda Craft

Snakes of the Amazon

Boa Constrictor
Boa B. constrictor

Green Anaconda
Eunectes murinus

Yellow Anaconda
Eunectes notaeus

 **South American Bushmaster**
 Lachesis muta

Snakes of the Amazon

Emerald Tree Boa
Corallus caninus

 **Fer-de-Lance**
Bothrops lanceolatus

Chicken Snake
Spilotes pullatus

 Green Vine Snake
Oxybelis fulgidus

Snakes of the Amazon

  **Tropical Rattlesnake**
Crotalus durissus

Rainbow Boa
Epicrates cenchria

 False Water Cobra
Hydrodynastes gigas

Amazon Whipsnake
Chironius carinatus

CLOTHESPIN PIRANHA

Instructions

The waters of the Amazon river are home to a rather intimidating fish, called the piranha. This potentially harmful fish inhabits South American rivers, floodplains, lakes and reservoirs. The name piranha comes from the indigenous Tupi people literally meaning "biting-fish". Although rare, these fish have been known to attack humans, especially children due to their splashing. Most attacks, however, are a single bite, and rarely cause significant injuries.

Color the included piranha illustration with crayons or markers. Cut out the fish and then cut in half following the dotted line and the serration of the teeth. Glue one side to the side of a clothespin. Allow to dry thoroughly. For faster results, use hot glue. Repeat for other side of illustration. Open and close the fish's mouth by manipulating the clothespin.

Materials

- Piranha Templates
- Scissors
- Crayons (or Markers)
- Clothespins
- Craft or Hot Glue

Clothespin Piranha

Counting Clip Cards

| 1 | 5 | 2 | 7 | 5 | 6 |

| 8 | 6 | 7 | 5 | 4 | 3 |

Counting Clip Cards

| 3 | 5 | 4 | 6 | 4 | 5 |

| 1 | 3 | 2 | 3 | 4 | 2 |

Counting Clip Cards

| 4 | 5 | 6 | 6 | 5 | 7 |

| 8 | 9 | 7 | 1 | 3 | 2 |

Counting Clip Cards

| 3 | 5 | 4 | 3 | 2 | 1 |

| 3 | 2 | 4 | 3 | 4 | 5 |

Brazil Currency
Brazilian Real R$

The Brazilian Real R$ is the main unit of Brazilian currency. The centavos is a subdivision worth 1/100 of a Real.

*This is a sample of some of the currency in circulation. Please note that some of the money depicted may be altered in size and detail, with illustrations including one side only to adhere to legal requirements regarding currency reproduction for educational and artistic use.

Brazil Currency
Brazilian Real R$

The Brazilian Real R$ is the main unit of Brazilian currency. The centavos is a subdivision worth 1/100 of a Real.

*This is a sample of some of the currency in circulation. Please note that some of the money depicted may be altered in size and detail, with illustrations including one side only to adhere to legal requirements regarding currency reproduction for educational and artistic use.

Brazil Currency
Brazilian Real R$

The Brazilian Real R$ is the main unit of Brazilian currency. The centavos is a subdivision worth 1/100 of a Real.

Centavos

This is a sample of some of the currency in circulation. Please note that some of the money depicted may be altered in size and detail, with illustrations including one side only to adhere to legal requirements regarding currency reproduction for educational and artistic use.

Indigenous Tribes of the Amazon

Awá

Guaraní

Kawahiva

Yanomami

Guaraní

The Guaraní are a group of culturally-related indigenous peoples of South America. They are distinguished from the related Tupi by their use of the Guarani language. They are one of the larger indigenous tribes of the Amazon, with approximately three million members.

The Guaraní have had a great cultural influence on the countries they inhabited. For instance, Brazil has numerous football teams named Guarani. Santo Ângelo Airport, in Santo Ângelo, Rio Grande do Sul, Brazil, is named after Sepé Tiaraju.

Awá

The Awá are an indigenous people of Brazil living in the Amazon rainforest. There are approximately 350 members, with almost a third having no contact with the outside world. They are considered endangered due to conflicts with logging interests in their territory.

The Awá people speak Guajá, a Tupi–Guaraní language. Originally living in settlements, they became nomadic around 1800 to avoid invasions by the Europeans.

Yanomami

The Yanomami, are a group of approximately 35,000 indigenous people who live in approximately 200–250 villages in the Amazon rainforest between Venezuela and Brazil.

Groups of Yanomami live in villages usually consisting of their children and extended families. Villages vary in size, but usually contain between 50 and 400 people. The men primarily do the hunting, while the women take care of the children and are responsible for many domestic duties. Yanomaman languages are comprised of four main varieties: Ninam, Sanumá, Waiká, and Yanomamö.

Kawahiva

The Kawahiva, formerly known as the Rio Pardo Indians, are an uncontacted indigenous tribe living near the Rio Pardo in the north of Mato Grosso, Brazil. They are nomadic people who have little contact with outsiders.

The Kawahiva live in communal shelters, using primitive spinning wheels to make string and make nets of tree bark. They are a hunting and gathering society, and rely on temporary hunting camps, not staying in one place for very long. It is believed that loggers have intentionally tried to keep the Kawahiva on the run.

Indigenous Tribes of the Amazon

Kayapo

Asháninka

Ingarikó

Kadiweu

Asháninka

The Asháninka are indigenous people living in the rainforests of Peru and in the State of Acre, Brazil.

The Asháninka grow yucca roots, sweet potato, corn, bananas, rice, coffee, cacao and sugar cane in biodiversity-friendly techniques. They also hunt and fish, primarily using bows and arrows or spears.

The Asháninka paint their faces in a variety of designs using the bright red crushed seeds of achiote fruits. For ceremonial purposes, the men also wear woven circles of palm leaves decorated with feathers on their heads.

Kayapo

Kayapo are indigenous people in Brazil who inhabit a vast area spreading across the states of Pará and Mato Grosso, south of the Amazon River and along Xingu River and its tributaries. The term "Kayapo" is used by neighboring groups rather than the Kayapo themselves.

These people live in villages consisting of huts. The Kayapo use intricate painted designs to covering their entire bodies (and sometimes used as decorations in their homes). They believe that their ancestors learned their social skills from insects, so they paint their bodies to mimic them and to better communicate with the Spirit that exists everywhere.

Kadiwéu

Also known as the 'índios cavaleiros' or 'horsemen Indians,' the Kadiwéu are members of a single surviving group of the Mbayá, The Mbayá were raiders in the 18th century and numbered 4,000, but smallpox and influenza radically decreased their population at the end of the 18th century.

A warrior people, they fought for Brazil in the Paraguayan War, an event that led to recognition of their lands. They currently live in a territory located in the State of Mato Grosso do Sul, including an area of the Pantanal. Today they are known for their horse riding skills and intricate face paintings.

Ingarikó

Ingarikó is a term that collectively refers to three closely related tribes of indigenous people known as the Akawaio, Pemon and Patamona people.

Kaieteur Falls is an important cultural site, named after Old Kaie, a member of the Patamona tribe.

For hunting, they traditionally use blowpipes or bows and arrows but nowadays they also use guns. They make a lot of different alcoholic and non-alcoholic drinks. Common agricultural products include bitter cassava, yam, sweet potato, sugarcane, chili pepper, squash. They also gather wild mushrooms for consumption and eat some insects.

Indigenous Tribes of the Amazon

Wai-wai

Wapichana

Dslala

Uncontacted

Wapichana

The Wapichana are an indigenous group found in the Roraima area of southern Guyana and northern Brazil. Early Wapishana settlements were temporary clusters of homes, but today they have become permanent villages usually surrounding a church. Cassava is an important crop for the Wapishana society. They also hunt deer, agouti, wild turkeys, and birds, and raise cattle, swine, chicken and ducks.

Joênia Wapixana, a member of the Wapixana tribe, became the first indigenous attorney in Brazil and first indigenous woman deputy elected to Brazilian National Congress.

Wai-wai

The Wai-wai are a Carib-speaking Indigenous people of Guyana and northern Brazil. Their society consists of different lowland forest peoples who have maintained much of their cultural identity.

The Wai Wai are known for their weaving. They twist cotton into yarn for weaving, and are known for their hammock weaving. All the hammocks are weaved on square hammock frames. They also create pottery, woven combs, bone flutes, and other crafts. Consuming primate meat is a source of pride for Wai-wai, distinguishing them as "true' forest people" and making them distinct from other indigenous groups.

Uncontacted

Brazil's Amazon is home to more uncontacted tribes than anywhere in the world. There are thought to be at least 100 isolated groups in this rainforest, according to the government's Indian affairs department FUNAI.

Very little is known about these people, but their decision to avoid contact with other tribes and outsiders is almost certainly a result of previous disastrous encounters and the ongoing invasion and destruction of their forest home. In addition, outside diseases have threatened many of these tribes, and in some cases decimated tribes entirely.

Dslala

The Dslala are an indigenous people of Brazil living in the lower Vale do Javari in the western Amazon Basin. They are commonly referred to as "Korubo" but this is a degrading, negative label given by a former enemy tribe and later adopted as a tribal designation by the outside world. Much of what the outside world knows of this group is based on the research of Brazilian explorer Sydney Possuelo, who first contacted the tribe in 1996

The Korubo are some of the last people on Earth to live in near-isolation from modern society, although they have, on numerous occasions, had violent contacts with the surrounding communities.

REDE HAMMOCK

Instructions

The Brazilian hammock is a legacy of aboriginal South America and Brazil. Indigenous native tribes considered the hammock not only a necessary accessory, as it was not just a utilitarian object, but also a feature of each race depending on the style and colors and a sign of social prestige depending on how large and elaborate the hammock they had.

Materials
- Weaving Template
- Scissors
- Hole Punch
- Assorted Yarn
- Crochet Hook/Large Blunt Needle

Cut out included weaving template; punch holes as indicated on both ends. Using a crochet hook or large blunt needle, thread 16 pieces of yarn through both ends, and tie securely on both ends. Using a contrasting color, secure to top of one side with a knot and weave back and forth to form a rough weave. If necessary, secure more thread to continue weaving by knotting ends together. Use multiple colors to create a colorful hammock. Continue until entire template is completed. Secure end with a knot and remove paper template. Hang from both ends and place a small doll or stuffed animal in it. **Discuss:** Have you ever laid on a hammock? Could you sleep on it all night? How does it feel different than your bed?

Kayapo Design Tracing

The Kayapo are known for their intricate designs; complete the designs and work on tracing skills using authentic Kayapo illustrations.

Kayapo Design Tracing

ASHÁNINKA PALM CROWN

Instructions

The Asháninka are indigenous peoples living in the rainforests of Peru and in the state of Acre, Brazil. They have a distinct physical style, including using the bright red crushed seeds of achiote fruit to decorate their faces and wearing woven circular crowns of palm leaves decorated with feathers on their heads.

Materials
- Palm Crown Cutout
- Scissors
- Tape
- Glue
- Feathers

Cut out included palm crown pieces with scissors. Glue or tape two circular pieces together along tabs, making sure pattern matches up. Secure the patterned rectangle pieces together at ends with glue and/or tape. Measure around child's head and trim to fit. Secure circular piece to crown with tape or glue. Punch holes on one side with hole punch. Insert colorful feathers into holes and glue to secure.

Discuss: What are some other kinds of iconic hats? What are they made of? What countries are they associated?

Asháninka Palm Crown

Asháninka Palm Crown

Asháninka Palm Crown

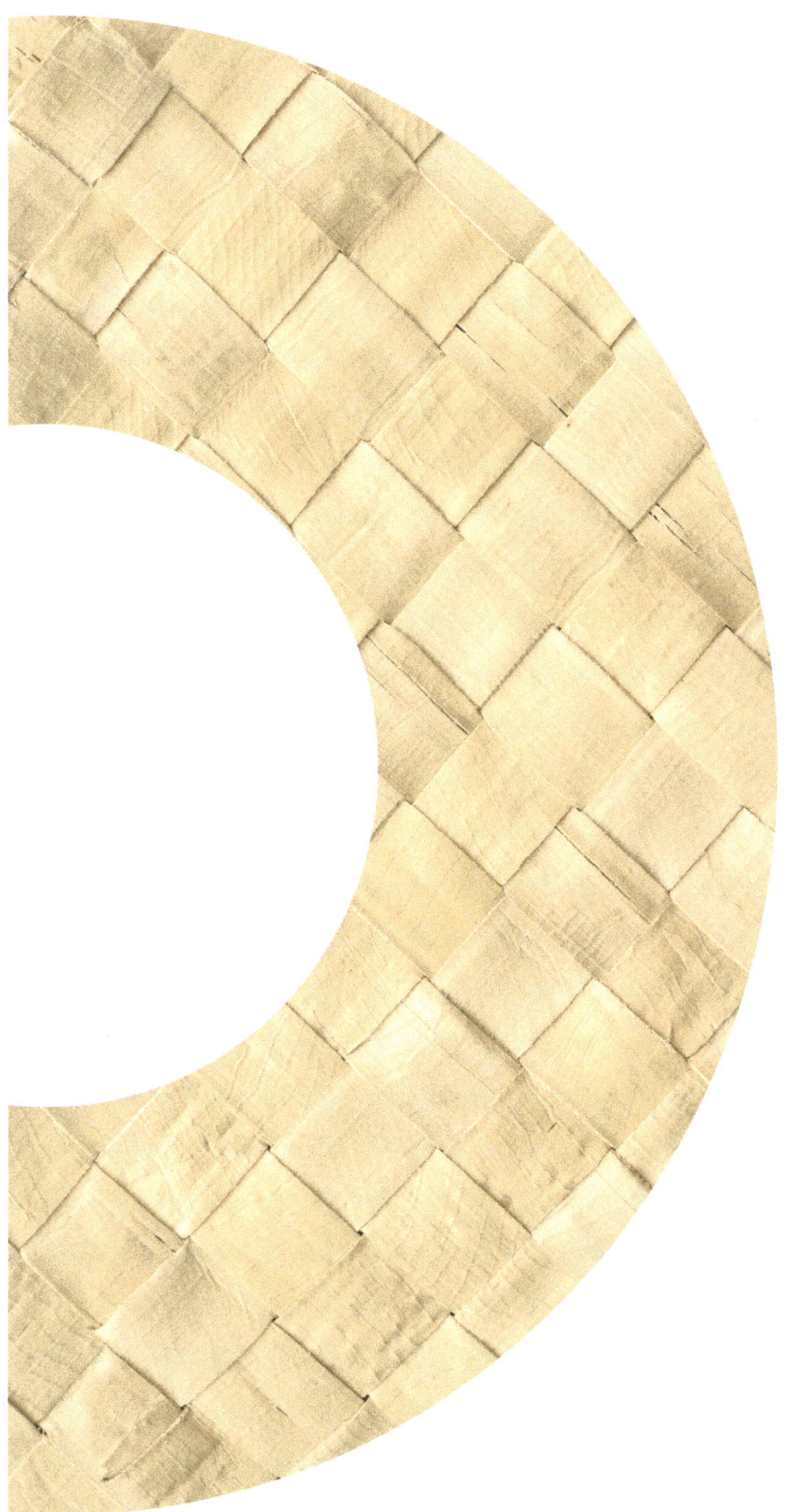

Savy Activities

Travel the world through the interactive learning activities of **Savy Activities**; these hands-on resources provide parents, caregivers and educators practical ways to teach children about the world around them. Each book features a country, location or time period where subjects such as geography, history, vocabulary, reading, language, science, mathematics, music and art come alive by engaging auditory, visual and kinesthetic learning styles.

All activity books include geography with applicable maps, landmarks and locations. Historical events and time periods are visually represented with full color posters and flashcards, if applicable. Each book includes a set of fun-fact cards, poster and flag, if applicable. Paper models allow children to create 3D creations of major landmarks and structures. All books include a life cycle and anatomy of a plant, animal or organic compound, with flashcards and 3-part cards featuring important structures applicable to the theme.

Children learn scientific principles through active experiments and activities. Traditional customs, festivals, toys, clothing and art are also explored. Each book includes an exclusive themed mini-story featuring historical events or traditional mythology and folklore to promote vocabulary and reading. Where applicable, world languages are introduced through engaging flashcards, posters and tracing work. Each country has been meticulously researched by interviewing native persons and/or personal travel experiences to ensure the authentic culture is fully explored.

Savy Activities utilizes concepts from multiple educational methods to create unique resources allowing children a tangible and enjoyable way to explore their world. The **Savy Activities** series should not be viewed as a curriculum, but rather complimentary thematic resources to enhance traditional education. Because the individual needs and knowledge of children varies within standardized grade levels, **Savy Activities** resources have the flexibility to be used with preschool learners through early to mid-elementary years. For younger learners, adult supervision and/or assistance may be needed and activities presented in a simplified version. For older learners, resources may be paired with additional content from other materials to meet learning outcomes.

Check out our other products and resources at **www.SavyActivities.com**